MW00776218

Maitz' artwork on the cover makes any book stand out from a shelf and yell "read me first!"

—*Anne McCaffrey*

Don Maitz is a fine talent in his field at this moment. Imagine what he will be doing in 2001!

—*Ray Bradbury*

I've been glad to have Don illustrating my books. Damn, he's good.

—*C.J. Cherryh*

Don Maitz has that rare visionary gleam that surprises us with a whole new way of looking at the world. Call them science fiction or fantasy if you like, but his pictures hold a wonderful magic mirror up to nature, juxtaposing the familiar and the unexpected into images that delight us with an irrepressible sense of fun. A triumph of imagination!

—*James Gurney*

Don Maitz is a top Fantasy and Science Fiction illustrator. Through books such as this one, everybody can share in his paintings. You will find some of the best contemporary art our field has to offer, by a recognized master of the form. So relax, read on, and enjoy.

—*Michael Whelan*

THE ART OF DON MAITZ

Dreamquests

Underwood-Miller
Novato, California
Lancaster, Pennsylvania

DREAMQUESTS
ISBN 0-88733-176-9 (softcover edition)
ISBN 0-88733-175-0 (cloth edition)

This copyright is valid in the United States and all nations of the International Copyright Union. All rights reserved. This book, or parts thereof, may not be reproduced in any form including electronic retrieval or storage systems without explicit permission of the copyright holders. For information address the publisher: Underwood-Miller, Inc., 708 Westover Drive, Lancaster, PA 17601.

Copyright © 1993 by Underwood-Miller, Inc.
Art copyright © 1993 by Don Maitz
Introduction copyright © 1993 by Ray Feist
Foreword copyright © 1993 by Don Maitz
Afterword copyright © 1993 by Janny Wurts

Cover design & book design by Arnie Fenner
Printed in Singapore

For further information regarding the artwork of Don Maitz, write to him at 5824 Bee Ridge Road; Suite 106, Sarasota, Florida 34233.

Selected images from the art collection of Don Maitz will be published as limited edition prints by Mill Pond Press, Inc., Venice, FL 34292. For more information or the name of your local Mill Pond Press dealer call 1-800-535-0331.

It Takes Courage poster is available, as well as a selection of fantasy greeting cards from this book and *First Maitz.* Contact Dragon Tales; P.O. Box 8007, The Woodlands, TX 77387

Forty Thieves pirate poster is available through the Greenwich Workshop. For the name of your local dealer contact (800) 243-4246; or write to the Greenwich Workshop; P.O. Box 393, Trumbull, CT 06611-0393

Magic Casement is offered as a signed a numbered lithograph. Contact The Fantasy Gallery; 416 Westheimer, Houston, TX 77006, (713) 528-6569

Trading cards of Don Maitz's work will be available from the Friedlander Publishing Group in early 1994.

Captain Morgan Original Spiced Rum/Puerto Rican Rum with spice and other natural flavors/70 Proof/a product of the Captain Morgan Rum Co./Baltimore, MD.

Library of Congress Cataloging-in-Publication Data
    Maitz, Don, 1953–
        Dreamquests : the art of Don Maitz
            p.   cm.
        ISBN 0-88733-175-0 (cloth edition) : @29.95. -- ISBN 0-88733-176-9 (softcover edition) : $17.95
            1. Maitz, Don, 1953-   --Science fiction--Illustrations. 2. Themes, motives.   3. Book jackets--United States. I. Title.
        NC1883.3.M35A4   1993
        741.6′4′092--dc20
                                                                    93-31733
                                                                        CIP

To Janny,
Dreamchaser, companion, and wife

and thanks to Arnie Fenner
for putting my best look forward

Acknowledgement

I would like to acknowledge: trees. No living entity has given more to make this book. In fact, my career as an artist has been built upon their very fiber. From the pencils and papers I use, the supports onto which I paint, the binders of my pigments, the mahl stick that keeps my knuckles from dragging, my brush handles, my easel, sketchbooks, research materials, frames, even to the walls that hang my pictures, I owe a debt of thanks to this natural resource that has given its all to my benefit. A great sacrifice has been made to put his book in your hands, but it was not mine. Promote an artist, plant a tree.

CONTENTS

For additional information about each painting please see the Artworks
Glossary at the back of this book.

I've known Don Maitz since 1983. Met him at the World Fantasy Convention in Chicago that year. I didn't know much about him, save he had done an illustration for my novel, *Magician*, that had been used in the Literary Guild Book Club catalog. I liked the painting; I bought it some years later. Anyway, I had a chance to chat with him a little, then at the end of the weekend, he introduced me to Janny Wurts. For those of you who don't know, she has since become my collaborator on three novels and Don's wife, in that order.

Due to my work with Janny, I've gotten to know Don pretty well over the years. Here are some of the boring facts: he was born and grew up someplace back in the East where the winters are lousy and you have to drive a long way to find decent skiing. This is significant, as Don is something of a sports junky. If he's not furiously painting, he's likely to be found windsurfing, sailing, horseback riding, or skiing. Don's childhood was boring. That's what he says anyway. I suspect those who knew him then would probably disagree, but I wasn't there, so I'll take him at his word. Besides, if you want to know about Don's childhood, you ask him.

Most of us are more interested in Don because of his work.

It's very good. In fact, it's among the best illustration being done in the world today. Don's the last person to ask about how good his work is, because he's self-deprecating and never happy. I don't know if that's the mark of a good artist or someone with a major personality disorder, but either way, if you ask Don about one of his paintings, he's likely to tell you what's wrong with it. Self-promotion is not one of his strong points.

Here's what Gene Wolfe has to say about Don's work, in his introduction to Don's first book, *First*

Maitz: "Don Maitz is a great cover artist because he creates images that attract your attention *and* make you want to study them more closely." Amen. I've had great covers that were lousy art. Don does great covers and great art. That's rare. Ask illustrators who among their own ranks they respect, and the list is short. It's the consistency and the ability to combine art with commercial power that we're discussing, and in that company, Don has few peers.

Don has painted ten covers for me, out of nine books I've written, which is a pretty good trick. Not all were first editions, or available in this country, but every one of them is among the very best I've gotten. I have never been unhappy with one of Don's works.

Why is he so darn good? Well, if I knew I'd bottle it and sell it. My best guess is that Don has a whacked sense of things that gives a sly humor to much of his work. There's a loopy quirkiness to his paintings that is unique. Even those paintings that appear mundane at first glance will contain elements that will continue to reveal themselves if one but takes the time to study them. His works on C.J. Cherryh's books spring to mind as examples of this. Don also loves detail; there's never a part of any work that's

left unfinished, vague, or ill-defined because it's "not important." That's not Don's style. He loves to "noodle," to put in tiny bits here and there that add tremendously to the wealth of the whole. His detail can be stunning at times and has been oft imitated by others, yet rarely matched. Whatever he has hanging will be worth a long inspection, because you can't tell all of his brilliance in a quick glance.

Other things you should know about Don Maitz: He is deaf in one ear, so if you're talking to him and he's ignoring you, it's not that he's being a rude sod. Walk around to the other side and repeat what you said; if he continues to ignore you, *then* he's being a rude sod. Don also has outrageous taste in neckties, and he loves bad puns. You were warned. Anyone engaging Don in puns does so at his or her own risk.

—*Raymond E. Feist*

DREAMQUESTS is a collection of what's "hanging around" with my name on it. For the past twenty years I have been seriously involved with fantasy art. Out of the pressures and deadlines of book publishing, I bring you images from the wild and wooly world of "what if."

Words have been used for centuries as a point of departure for artists' perceptions. The inspiration for many great works originated from literature. The Sistine Chapel ceiling, the Last Supper, along with masters' works in hundreds of museums, and of course, the countless memorable publications with accompanying pictures that all have artwork derived from someone's written thoughts.

This ability to portray an invisible thought or dream is what this book is about, be they the artist's thoughts and dreams being represented for themselves, or a painted interpretation drawn from an author's written text. Most artists interpret the world around them visually. Fantasy art requires them to use their mind's eye as well. There is nothing like a good imaginative story to give a painting depth and purpose and to give visual wings to dreams.

It is said that fantasy is the language of dreams. Dreams can express facets of reality with direct and focused poignancy. The heart and soul of any subject can be expressed with no baggage of prejudice and few barriers between cultures because beauty and mystery are universal.

We all carry our emotions with us. Often they are physically expressed, written into our expressions. The majority of these feelings are subtle and deep within us, but they can be triggered or directed by a picture. Responses may vary in each individual, but emotions are common to us all. I try to reach out through my paintings, to tap this universal language. By manipulating the colors, shapes, textures, lines, and intensity of the elements, I hope to create mood and movement. Activity, conflict, and harmony are orchestrated to provide a form of music for the eyes where I control the volume and the impact. The characters, scenes, costumes, and details are designed to intensify the experience so as to draw in the onlooker and capture them in the moment. The challenge is always to portray and bring out intangible things like pride, adventure, happiness, mistrust, greed, or sorrow through imagery. I enjoy realistic renditions that invite exploration, that suggest something beyond what is physically revealed, and that push buttons and create a reaction.

As you look through these pages, you may see something personal in one of my works that you identify with. I may not have consciously planned your exact response but, if you should ask if that identification was intentional, I would say, of course, that I planned it all along. You see, in a sense I did because the work was designed to affect you.

The first impression of an art book is its cover. DREAMQUESTS' title evolved as a representative and expressive word that exemplifies the thrust of my work. The best image to portray that concept, as this book's cover, seemed exemplified by a painting of mine produced several years ago. Since the elements in that piece were made for a more vertical format, not to mention being an older work already reproduced within my past art book *First Maitz,* I decided to revise the work, updating and deepening the scope of the art for its new specific purpose. My more recent experience with horses and hawks provided a unique opportunity to improve upon the original elements. Indeed, it seemed I had been collecting research materials unconsciously just for this painting.

The paired figures represent opposite attitudes. One is shown in flight, pursuing his dreams, while the other waits passively, wishing her dreams might come true. To symbolize these ideas I used the feather as a repeating element. "On the wings of a dream," and "flights of fancy" were two phrases that sprang to mind, and the flying horse, being dream, and the white feathers, being fanciful decorations, lend atmosphere to these concepts. The peacock feathers and the bird they derive from represent the artist's natural instinct to show off his colors and to attract attention. In having this collection of my work reproduced here, I feel very much like the peacock. My colorful mind's eye plumage is spread open with the pages to attract and hopefully to affect you. I am hoping you will discover an imaginative adventure where the surface image will reveal an inner landscape and a story untold—a window into another world that only an artist can provide.

—*Don Maitz*

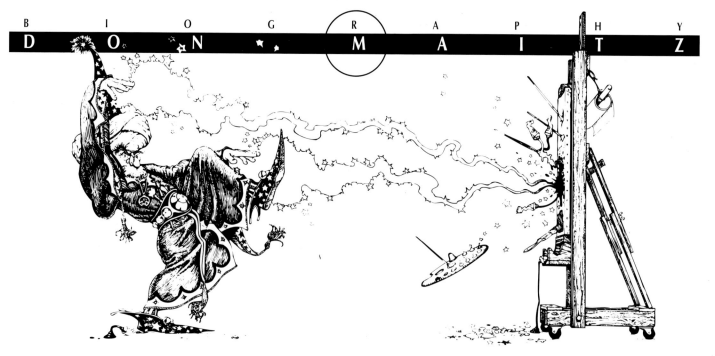

Born on June 10, 1953 in Bristol, Connecticut, Don Maitz has been actively engaged in artistic pursuits since childhood. He attended the University of Hartford's evening figure drawing class while in his final year at Plainville High School. Upon graduation he entered the Paier School of Art in Hamden, Connecticut where he graduated "Top of the Class" in 1975.

An award winning illustrator, Maitz has achieved international acclaim for his book cover paintings and commissions, which now number over two hundred and fifty, specializing in fantasy and science fiction imagery. His work has also appeared as poster, greeting card, jigsaw puzzle, and record album reproductions. His most widely distributed and most recognizable image is the pirate for Captain Morgan Spiced Rum.

Nearly every year since his work entered the marketplace, Don has been nominated for the premier award in his chosen field. In 1990 he received a special Best Original Artwork Award. In 1990 and 1993 he received the Hugo Award for Best Artist. His previous art book *First Maitz* was a nominee in the Non-Fiction Hugo category. Maitz was also presented the Howard Award for Best Artist at the sixth World Fantasy Convention. By peer vote, he has received eight Chesley Awards from the Association of Science Fiction and Fantasy Artists (ASFA). In 1980 the Society of Illustrators honored him with the Silver Medal Award of Excellence and more recently he was given a certificate of merit for his *Forty Thieves,* a painting of a shipload of pirates. These two awards originate from the Society's Annual Competition and were juried from approximately six thousand entries.

Committed to promoting fantasy illustration as a fine art form, Maitz was the driving force in organizing the first major exhibition of fantasy and science fiction art at an American museum. The showing, in 1980, at the New Britain Museum of American Art in Connecticut, broke all their previous attendance records. Maitz paintings were featured in later successful fantasy exhibitions at the Delaware Art Museum in Wilmington, and in NASA's 25th Anniversary exhibit, housed at the Cleveland Museum of Natural History. In New York City, his work has appeared in exhibitions at the Society of Illustrators, the Lever House, Park Avenue Atrium, and Hayden Planetarium. His work traveled in other exhibitions with stops at such locations as Brigham Young University and Orlando Science Center, and Worcester Museum. Two of his paintings reside in collections at the Delaware Art Museum and the New Britain Museum of American Art.

Countless genre related conventions have featured Don Maitz and his works; he has lectured at universities, and served a full term as a guest instructor of illustration at the Ringling School of Art and Design in Sarasota, Florida.

Currently, he is concentrating on images he has wanted to paint for some time and a series of fantasy paintings for a program of limited edition prints by Mill Pond Press, Venice, Florida; as well as his usual illustration commissions.

THE ART OF DON MAITZ

Dreamquests

© Don Maitz '78

© Don Maitz 78

19

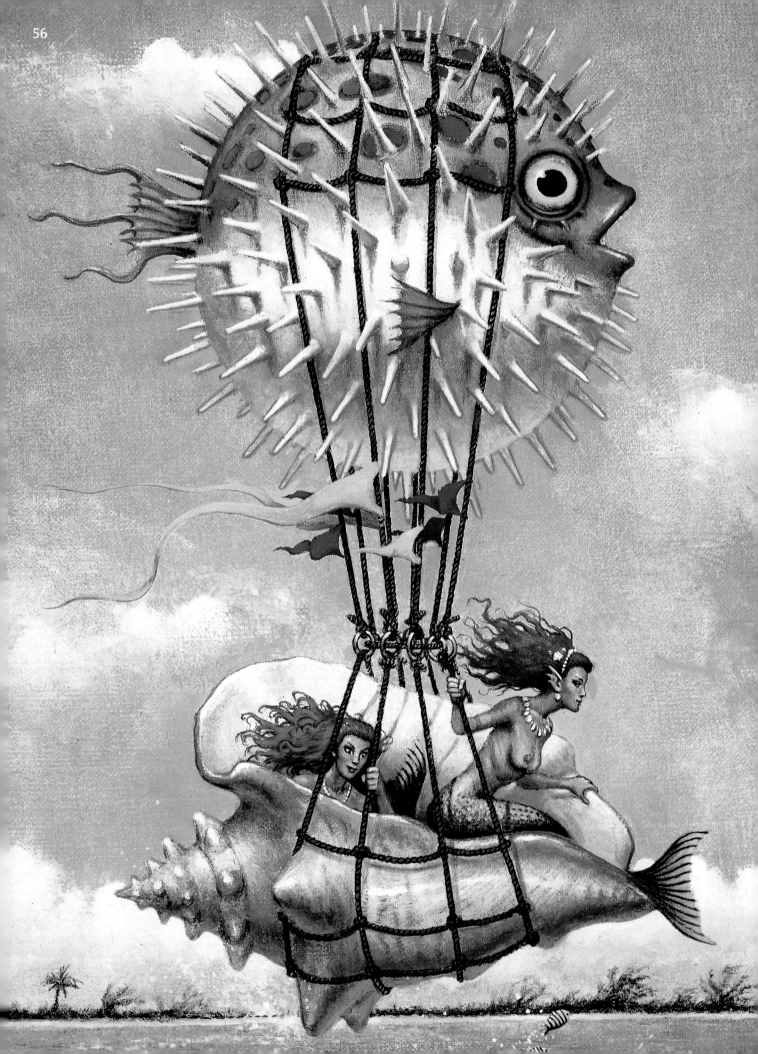

Maitz

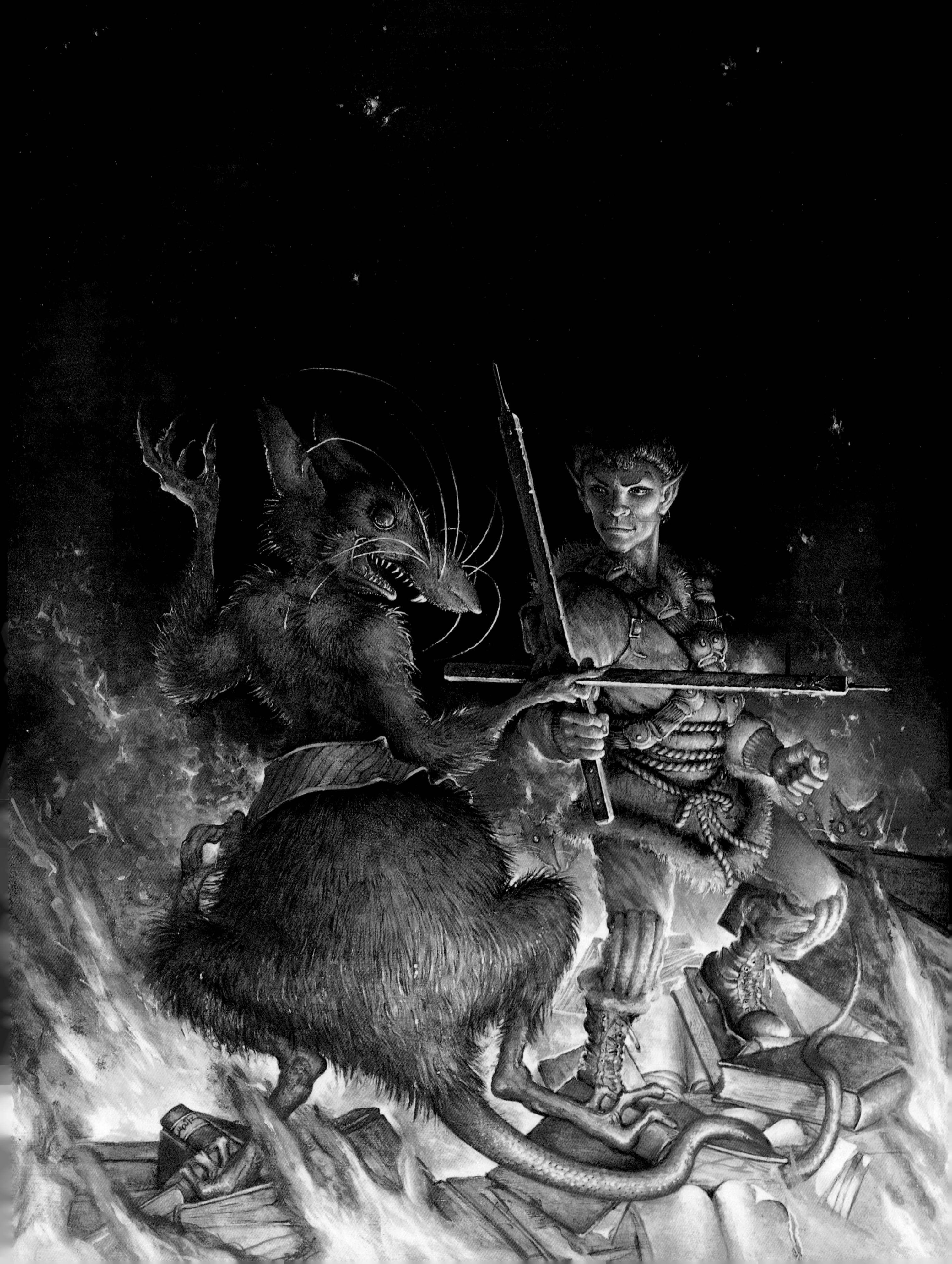

LEPRECHAU
ELVES
COVER ART BY Maitz
JODY'S GREMLIN J. NYE
BRIAN THOMSEN
ART DIRECTING BY DON PUCKEY
CONSULTING BILL FAWCETT

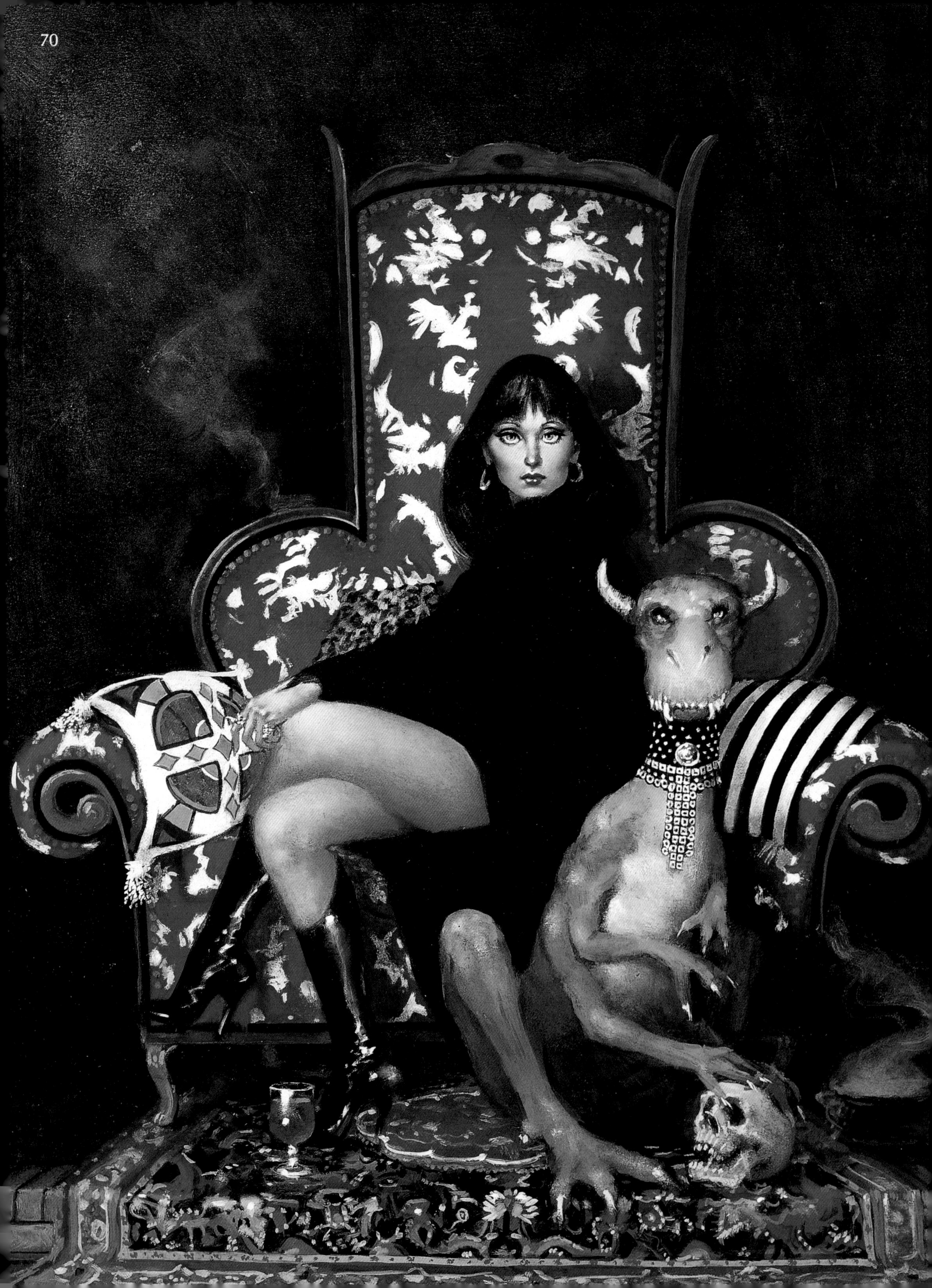

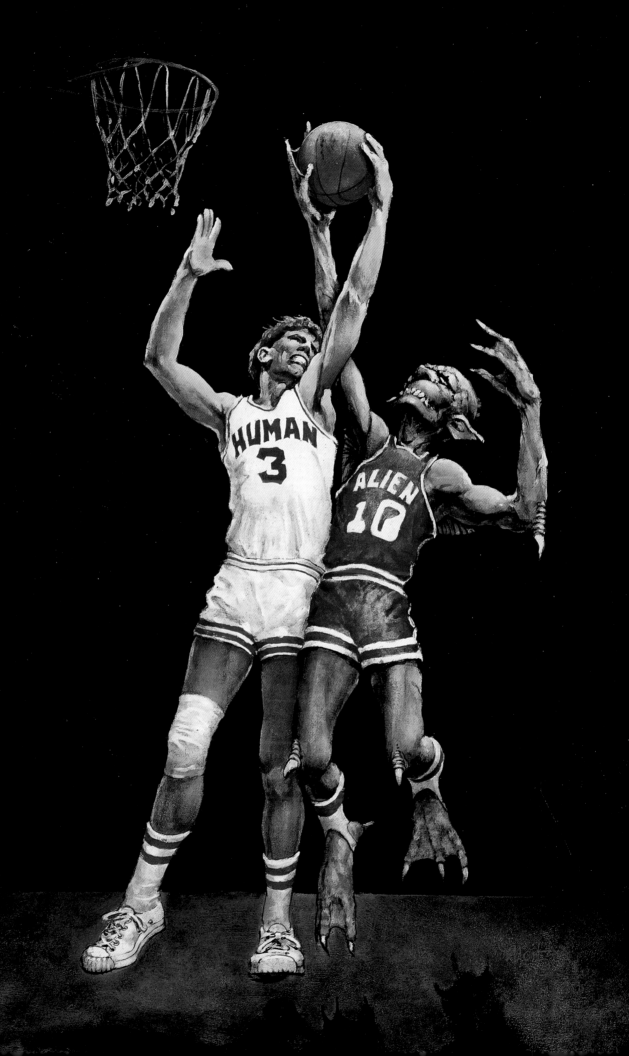

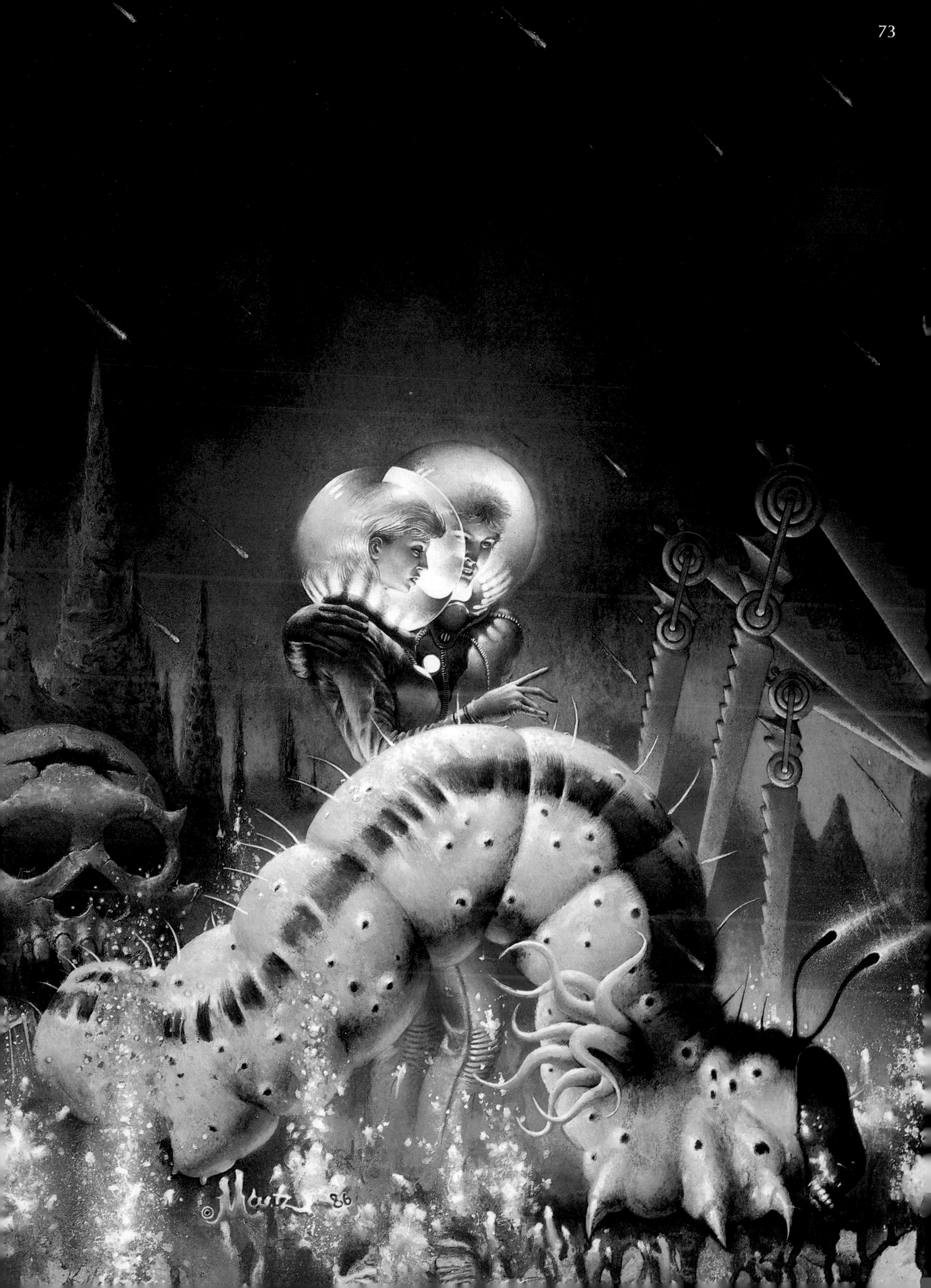
©Maitz 86

Don Maitz

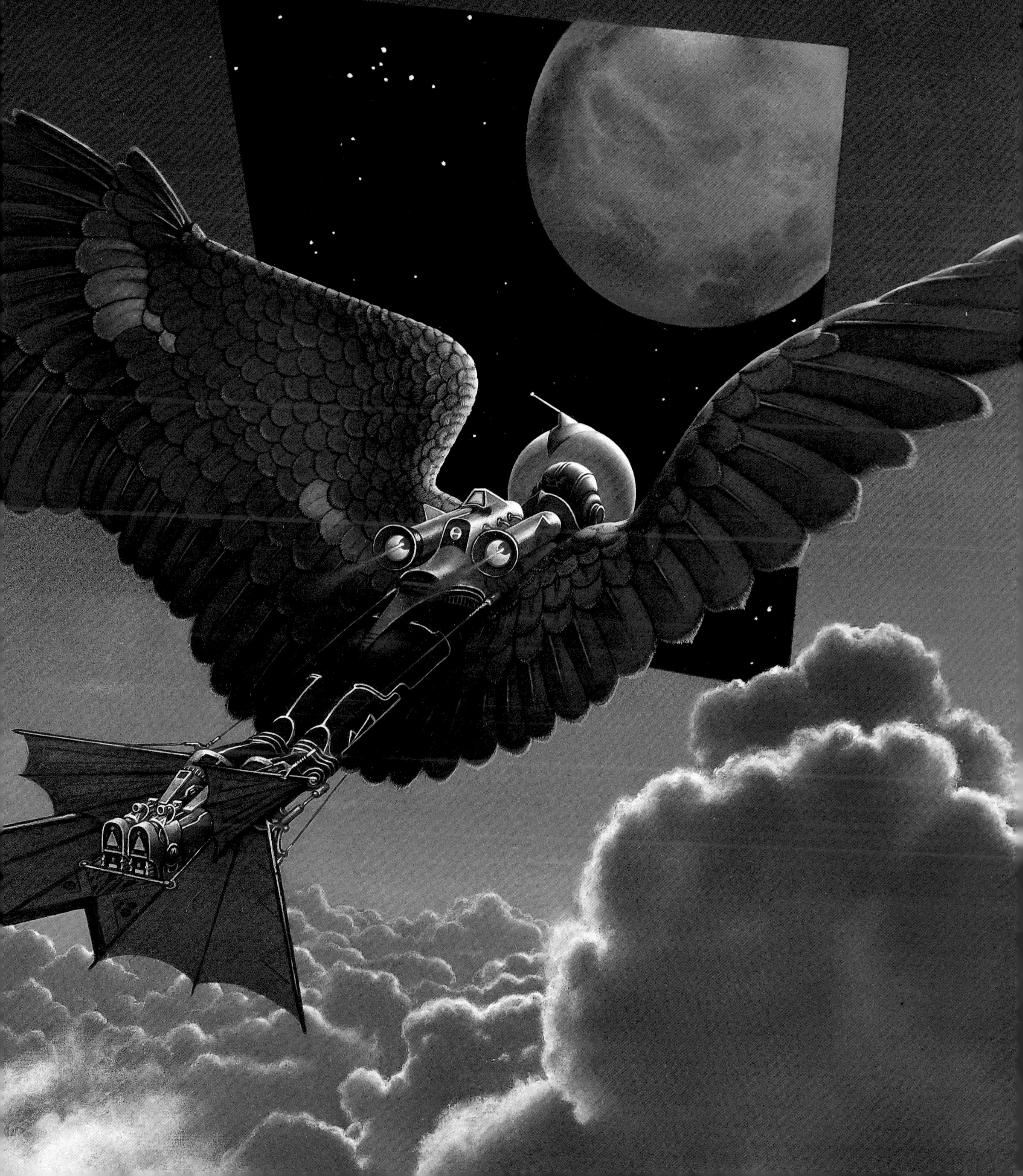

It's magic, the way Don paints; pure wizardry. There is no other way to explain it without dismantling the laws of physical science.

I first saw Don's work in *Tomorrow and Beyond*, a collection of works done by contemporary fantasy and science fiction illustrators. Among many artists, Don's works stood out, so much that I recalled his name. I met him at the World Fantasy Convention art show in Providence 1979. The moment remains very clear— I was standing, entranced and speechless, in front of his original painting, *The Second Drowning*. The tragic and romantic elements in the work stopped thought for twenty minutes. When I began to recover, to re-emerge from the moment into which his power had pulled me, I looked to my left, and lo, the fellow in the plaid shirt had a nametag on that said "Maitz."

Well, I confess I couldn't contain myself. I gushed out exactly what I thought of his work—and he just walked away, not saying anything.

It wasn't until a year later that I learned I'd spoken to his deaf ear—he hadn't heard one single word of anything I'd said. A tribute to his work, indeed, that I dared try to speak to him again.

Since, I've come to share a studio with Don, and a wonderful life. I've seen all aspects of how he creates— from his messily scribbled sketches, to the painstaking final drawings, to the agonies he goes through, and the stereo blasting all-nighters, to get each detail right.

As many times as I've watched the process, I still have no handle on how he does it—inexcusable, one would think, since I happen also to be an artist. But it's true. He has his own way, and whether his is a madman's creativity, or we, the sane beings too dull to comprehend his genius—he

gets things out of mere paints and paper that continually astound.

I've picked up his brushes—they keep their secrets unto frustration. They're more often than not beaten bushy; trashed, in plain language, to the point where any serious artist would fling them in the garbage with no compunction. He takes these things and does fine, fine, straight lines and ellipses with them. Magic. Hairs sticking out wild and sideways, and somehow no mark goes astray.

He paints and *paints* and PAINTS over areas where I can't see what's wrong. His eye sees beyond what mine sees, into a dream that's only his. I can only stand in awe of the effort and the hours, and know he's earned his success.

Not only brushes—Don uses anything that comes to hand; old doilies collected from restaurants, bits of aluminum screening, sponges, saran wrap, old socks, and yes, truly, once the toilet seat did not escape use as a template. Household items and kitchen utensils that vanish have a habit of turning up in the studio. If I didn't hate to cook so much, it might be a trial being his wife.

I have also been in the unique position of being an author that Don has illustrated. He did the cover paintings

for the Empire books I wrote in collaboration with Raymond Feist. His depiction of the characters, the mood, the reflected essence of the story, is uncanny in its perfection. I know what those story people looked like— and they came alive before my eyes out of somebody else's paintbrush. Magic. Wizardry.

Both are alive in Maitz's studio and imagination, as this book is tangible proof.

—*Janny Wurts*

Page ii: **Perilous Seas,** 8/90
Medium: acrylic/oil/masonite, 30" x 20"
For: Perilous Seas, Dave Duncan,
   Ballantine/Del Rey

Page vi: **Claws,** 9/82
Medium: oil/masonite, 29" x 20"
For: World Fantasy Convention Pro-
   gram Book (cover)
Unpublished

Page viii: **Conjure Maitz,** 12/87
Medium: oil/masonite, 30" x 30"
For: Cover of *First Maitz* 1988, promo-
   tional piece

Page x: **Dreamquest,** 7/93
Medium: oil/masonite, 30" x 22½"
For: Dreamquests, Don Maitz, Under-
   wood-Miller

Page 2–3: **Magician,** 10/91
Medium: oil/masonite, 22½" x 30"
For: Magician, Raymond E. Feist, Ban-
   tam Books
*Available as a limited edition from Mill
Pond Press*

Page 4: **Escape from Below,** 3/89
Medium: oil/masonite, 30" x 20"
For: Sunset Warrior, Eric von Lustbader,
   Fawcett (Ballantine/Del Rey)

Page 5: **After the Beast,** 4/89
Medium: oil/masonite, 30" x 20"
For: Shallows of Night, Eric von Lustba-
   der, Fawcett (Ballantine/Del Rey)

Page 6: **Kai-Feng,** 6/89
Medium: oil/masonite, 30" x 20"
For: Dai-San, Eric von Lustbader,
   Fawcett

Page 7: **Going for the Throat,** 8/89
Medium: oil/masonite, 30" x 20"
For: Beneath an Opal Moon, Eric von
   Lustbader, Fawcett

Page 8–9: **Beneath an Opal
   Moon,** 7/81
Medium: Acrylic/masonite, 21" x 28"
For: Beneath an Opal Moon, Eric von
   Lustbader, Fawcett

Page 10–11: **The Lion of Ireland,**
   11/80
Medium: oil/masonite, 28" x 38"
For: Lion of Ireland, Morgan Llywellyn,
   Playboy Press
Private Collection

Page 12: **Red Branch,** 9/88
Medium: oil/masonite, 24" x 20"
For: Red Branch, Morgan Llywellyn,
   William Morrow Co., Inc.

Page 13: **Arthur's Discovery,** 1975
Medium: oil/canvas board, 28" x 17"
For: unpublished
Private Collection

Page 14–15: **Divine Queen,** 12/81
Acrylic/masonite, 20" x 27"
For: The Divine Queen, Adam Corby,
   PocketBooks

Page 16–17: **Bring Me the Head
   of Prince Charming,** 3/91
Medium: oil/masonite, 20" x 27"
*For: Bring Me the Head of Prince
   Charming,* Roger Zelazny & Robert
   Sheckley, Bantam Books

Page 18: **Unsafe Footing,** 1977
Medium: oil/masonite, 24" x 18"
For: Creepy #94, Warren Publications
Reproductions: Greeting Card, Dragon
   Tales, 1989

Page 19: **Checkout the Sunset,**
   1978
Medium: oil/canvas, 27" x 17"
For: The City of the Sun, Brian M.
   Stableford, DAW
Private Collection

Page 20: **Knight at Sunset,** 10/91
Medium: oil/canvas, 26" x 18"
For: Unpublished

Page 21: **It Takes Courage,** 7/84
Medium: oil/masonite, 30" x 20"
For: Witchdame, Kathleen Sky, Berkley
Reproductions: First Maitz, Ursus Im-
   prints. 1988; Poster, Dragon Tales

Page 22: **The Oracle,** 11/88
Medium: oil/masonite, 30" x 20"
For: The Oracle, Hugh Cook, Warner
   Books

Page 23: **The Hero's Return,** 2/88
Medium: oil/masonite, 30" x 20"
For: The Hero's Return, Hugh Cook,
   Warner Books

Page 24: **Sleeping Beauty,** 4/82
Medium: acrylic/masonite, 20" x 20"
For: Parke Davis, Sudler & Hennessey
Private Collection

Page 24: **Rumpelstiltskin,** 5/82
Medium: acrylic/oil/masonite, 20" x 20"
For: Parke Davis, Sudler & Hennessey
Private Collection

Page 25: **Soldiers of Paradise,**
1/88
Medium: acrylic/masonite, 20" x 20"
For: Soldiers of Paradise, Paul Park,
   Arbor House

Page 26–27: **Daughter of the
   Empire,** 6/91
Medium: acrylic/oil/masonite, 24" x 36"
For: Daughter of the Empire, Raymond E.
   Feist & Janny Wurts, Bantam Books

Page 28–29: **Servant of the
   Empire,** 3/90
Medium: acrylic/oil/masonite, 24" x 36"
For: Mistress of the Empire, Raymond E.
   Feist & Janny Wurts, Bantam Books

Page 30–31: **Mistress of the Empire,** 8/91
Medium: acrylic/oil/masonite, 24" x 36"
For: Mistress of the Empire, Raymond E. Feist & Janny Wurts, Bantam Books

Page 32: **Wizard's Revenge,** 11/84
Medium: oil/masonite, 30" x 19"
For: In the Caverns of the Kalte, Book 2 of Lone Wolf Series, Putnam
Reproductions: Greeting Card, Dragon Tales
Private Collection

Page 33: **Urine Trouble with the King,** 3/81
Medium: oil/masonite, 30" x 20"
For: Dragons of Darkness, Edited by Orson Scott Card, Ace Books

Page 34: **Balance of Power,** 1978
Medium: oil/canvas, 28" x 18"
For: Balance of Power, Brian M. Stableford, DAW
In the Collection of the New Britain Museum of American Art

Page 35: **The Crusade,** 1978
Medium: oil/masonite, 29" x 17"
For: Camelot In Orbit, Arthur H. Landis, DAW
Reproductions: Jigsaw puzzle, Germany

Page 36: **The Magic Casement,** 12/89
Medium: acrylic/oil/masonite, 30" x 20"
For: The Magic Casement, Dave Duncan, Ballantine/Del Rey

Page 37: **Faery Lands Forlorn,** 6/90
Medium: acrylic/oil/masonite, 30" x 20"
For: Faery Lands Forlorn, Dave Duncan, Ballantine Books

Page 38: **Emperor & the Clown,** 4/91
Medium: oil/masonite, 30" x 20"
For: Emperor & the Clown, Dave Duncan, Ballantine/Del Rey

Page 39: **Conjure Mice,** 6/93
Medium: oil/masonite, 30" x 20"
For: Stranger at the Wedding, Barbara Hambly, Ballantine

Page 40–41: **Silverthorn,** 12/91
Medium: oil/masonite, 221/2" x 30"
For: Silverthorn, Raymond E. Feist, Bantam Books
Available as a limited edition from Mill Pond Press

Page 42–43: **Darkness at Sethanon,** 5/92
Medium: alkyd/masonite, 221/2" x 30"
For: A Darkness at Sethanon, Raymond E. Feist, Bantam Books

Page 44–45: **Prince of the Blood,** 6/92
Medium: oil/masonite, 221/2" x 30"
For: Prince of the Blood, Raymond E. Feist, Bantam Books

Page 46–47: **King's Buccaneer,** 2/92
Medium: oil/masonite, 221/2" x 30"
For: King's Buccaneer, Raymond E. Feist, Bantam Books

Page 48: **Treasure Cave,** 1/93
Medium: oil/masonite, 11" x 83/4"
For: Masterworks Miniature Show, Gallery One/Akron & Mentor, Ohio. Unpublished

Page 49: **No Prey, No Pay,** 5/93
Medium: oil/canvas, 40" x 36"
For: Unpublished

Page 50–51: **Forty Thieves,** 1/91
Medium: oil/masonite, 40" x 84"
For: Forty Thieves, Greenwich Workshop, Inc.
Reproductions: Fine Arts Poster, Greenwich Workshop

Page 52: **Captain Morgan in Rigging,** 4/92
Medium: acrylic/masonite, 231/2" x 351/2"
For: Seagram & Sons, DB Needham

Page 53: **Blood and Thunder,** 1/88
Medium: oil/canvas, 28" x 26"
For: Unpublished

Page 54–55: **Unknown Shores,** 10/92
Medium: acrylic/masonite, 20" x 27"
For: Unpublished
Available as a limited edition from Mill Pond Press

Page 56: **Tropical Fantasy,** 12/86
Medium: acrylic/canvas, 15" x 11"
For: Unpublished
Reproductions: Greeting Card, Dragon Tales, 1989
Private Collection

Page 57: **Sorcerer's Lady,** 9/85
Medium: oil/masonite, 30" x 20"
For: Sorcerer's Lady, Paula Volsky, Berkley

Page 58: **The Vampire Twins,** 1977
Medium: oil/masonite, 24" x 18"
For: Eerie #93, Warren Publications
In the Collection of the Delaware Art Museum

Page 59: **Greetings from the Otherworld,** 10/79
Medium: oil/masonite, 30" x 20"
For: Unpublished

Page 60: **Channel's Destiny,** 6/83
Medium: oil/masonite, 30" x 20"
For: Channel's Destiny, Jean Lorrah & Jacqueline Lichtenberg, DAW
Private Collection

Page 61: **The Grim Reaper in Purgatory,** 11/80
Medium: acrylic/masonite, 30" x 20"
For: First published in *First Maitz*
Private Collection

Page 62: **The Leap,** 9/81
Medium: oil/masonite, 30" x 20"
For: Book of the Beast, Robert Stallman, Pocketbooks

Page 63: **The Serenade,** 10/84
Medium: oil/masonite, 30" x 20"
For: Last Days at the Edge of the World,
   Brian Stableford, Berkley
Private Collection

Page 64–65: **The Perils,** 4/84
Medium: acrylic/masonite, 20" x 26"
For: The Talisman, Steven King/Peter
   Straub, Donald W. Grant

Page 66: **Borribles,** 11/83
Medium: acrylic/masonite, 30" x 20"
For: Borribles Across the Dark Metropolis,
   Michael DeLarrabeiti, Berkley
Private Collection

Page 67: **Borribles Across the
   Metropolis,** 8/87
Medium: acrylic/masonite, 24" x 17"
For: Borribles Across the Metropolis,
   Michael DeLarrabeiti, Berkley

Page 68: **Goon in the Kitchen,** 11/86
Medium: acrylic/masonite, 26" x 20"
For: Archer's Goon, Diana Wynne
   Jones, Berkley

Page 69: **Mythology 101,** 7/89
Medium: oil/masonite, 24" x 16"
For: Mythology 101, Jody Lynn Nye,
   Warner Books
Private Collection

Page 70: **Lady and Her Pet,** 1978
Medium: oil/illustration board, 27" x 20"
For: Back cover of the World Fantasy
   Con '82 program, 1982
Reproductions: Print, gift to artist from
   WFC, 1984; *First Maitz* b/w, Ursus
   Imprints, 1988

Page 71: **Aliens-10 Humans-3,**
1977
Medium: oil/illustration board, 25" x 21"
For: Eerie #88, Warren Publications
Private Collection

Page 72: **Triple Detente,** 2/86
Medium: acrylic/masonite, 24" x 20"
For: Triple Detente, Piers Anthony, Tor Books

Page 73: **E.S.P. Worm,** 2/86
Medium: acrylic, masonite, 26" x 20"
For: E.S.P. Worm, Piers Anthony, Tor
Books

Page 74–75: **The Island of Dr.
   Death,** 12/79
Medium: oil/masonite, 24" x 32"
*For: The Island of Dr. Death and Other
   Stories,* Gene Wolfe, Pocketbooks
Private Collection

Page 76: **Return to Doomstar,**
3/85
Medium: acrylic/masonite, 20" x 30"
For: Return to Doomstar, Richard Mey-
   ers, Warner Books

Page 77: **Pokerface,** 1977
Medium: oil/masonite, 24" x 16"
For: The Grand Wheel, Barrington J.
   Bayley, DAW
Private Collection

Page 78: **The Pretender,** 8/84
Medium: oil/masonite, 26" x 20"
For: The Pretender, Piers Anthony, Tor
   Books

Page 79: **The Hot Sleep,** 12/82
Medium: oil/masonite, 30" x 20"
For: The Worthington Chronicle, Orson
   Scott Card, Berkley

Page 80: **Out of the Blue,** 3/93
Medium: oil/masonite, 30" x 20"
For: The Losers, David Eddings, Ballant-
   ine Books

Page 81: **Catchworld,** 1978
Medium: oil/masonite, 30" x 20"
For: Catchworld, Chris Boyce, Fawcett

Page 82–83: **Empire Fleet Trans-
   port,** 1977
Medium: acrylic/masonite, 19½" x 28"
For: Rude Astronauts, Allen Steele, John
   Hopkins University Press, 1993

Page 84: **The Big Sun of
   Mercury,** 1977
Medium: acrylic/masonite, 24" x 16"
*For: Lucky Starr & the Big Sun of
   Murcury,* Isaac Asimov writing as
   Paul French, Fawcett

Page 85: **Spaced-Man,** 3/79
Medium: acrylic/masonite, 30" x 20"
For: Beyond Apollo, Barry Malzberg,
   Pocketbooks

Page 86: **Night Raid,** 4/81
Medium: acrylic/masonite, 30" x 20"
For: Assault on the Gods, Stephen
   Goldin, Fawcett

Page 87: **Hellburner,** 4/92
Medium: acrylic/masonite, 18" x 22"
For: Hellburner, C. J. Cherryh, Warner
   Books

Page 88: **Heavy Time,** 10/90
Medium: acrylic/masonite, 24" x 20"
For: Heavy Time, C. J. Cherryh, Warner
   Books

Page 89: **Rimrunners,** 9/88
Medium: acrylic/masonite, 30" x 20"
For: Rimrunners, C. J. Cherryh, Warner
   Books

Page 90: **Cyteen II,** 7/88
Medium: acrylic/masonite, 24" x 16"
For: Cyteen II, C. J. Cherryh, Warner
   Books

Page 91: **Cyteen III,** 7/88
Medium: acrylic/masonite, 24" x 16"
For: Cyteen III, C. J. Cherryh, Warner
   Books

Page 92–93: **Over the Clouds,**
12/88
Medium: oil/masonite, 18" x 30"
For: Classic Stories 2, Ray Bradbury,
   Bantam Books